Maha Al Maazmi is a young girl experiencing life, she gained friends and lost some. She went through many lessons in life but one thing mainly stuck in her mind, "trusting yourself is safer than trusting others."

To all the teenagers battling life.

Maha Al Maazmi

THE THOUGHTS OF A TEENAGER

AUSTIN MACAULEY PUBLISHERS™

LONDON • CAMBRIDGE • NEW YORK • SHARJAH

ISBN 9789948774563 (Paperback)
ISBN 9789948774556 (E-Book)

Application Number: MC-10-01-8342850
Age Classification: 13+

First Published 2024
AUSTIN MACAULEY PUBLISHERS FZE
Sharjah Publishing City
P.O Box [519201]
Sharjah, UAE
www.austinmacauley.ae
+971 655 95 202

This book is something I never expected to happen, but with the help of Austin Macauley Publishers and the support of my dear mother, it happened. It's simply like my biggest dream has come true. I would just like to say how strong someone's words can affect others in many ways we didn't know of, as well as how support is very important in every individual's life, and I am glad and truly grateful to have a mother who supported me through everything in my life. Thank you, Mom, because without you I wouldn't have accomplished what I have today.

Dear Mother

You are the shining star when it comes to light
you are the best person in my life
Despite the love hidden inside, you shined like a diamond in
the sky
You are a flower that makes me smile
your heart is filled with love and never had a whole, despite
my actions toward you sometimes
I love you deep down inside, you make me happy and
worth being alive
I love you forever and forever is a never-ending fairy tale
with a queen like you by my side
you are a strong woman hiding inside a hurt angel, she will
cry and shed tears when I'm not there to sigh along with her
fears.

Judgment

In Today's Society, no one can feel good in their own body,
feeling ashamed, worthless, and nothing but pain.
Even loving themselves and their body for who they are is a
problem,
a problem that society always invades,
getting into people's problems as if it's in their own vain.

Virus

Just because of a virus, I am stuck with the violence of
missing you day and night,
stuck with the thought of not having the ability to see you,
stuck with the thought of being alone in this era without you
in my eye sight,
being stuck without the ability of movement when you are
not there by my side,
missing your love and affection that has always been with
me.

Covid

Thanks to covid,
we are stuck home with a thought that will never leave us
alone,
day and night always thinking about you but never having a
clue why I am missing you,
thinking of what I should do when I am clueless when the
pain will go through,
being here without you is something I didn't wish to go
through.

Disappointment or Satisfaction

Words can't describe how I feel at the moment,
a bit of everything all at once,
disappointment is what I attract, but satisfaction is what I
need.
I need to feel satisfied with whom I am,
satisfaction doesn't come as fast as disappointment,
it's like a simple race.
Who wins first… disappointment or satisfaction?
Yet somehow disappointment always gets its way in
winning!

Responsibility

Responsibility isn't a game,
it teaches you how to be a real man,
it's not a game to play with, it's your whole life to depend
on, you might hate it but you can't run away from it,
it teaches you to be independent and confident,
it's the reason why this world is organized because everyone
has their own mind and duty,
it doesn't allow you to break the rules or be a bully that's
going through life too,
it gives you the strength and courage to do what people
always have to do.
At some point in your life, you're going to be responsible for
not only yourself but for your loved ones too,
it's a cycle of life, you got to do what you must do,
you can't stop it but you can own it and be responsible.

Loss

Losing you was a hard, traumatic experience,
being around you after, it was harder…
someone who made me cry…
caused me such disaster…
made me someone who i am not…
giving my heart to someone was a mistake i did but will
never repeat,
a heart has been broken once and it will never be the same,
it will never love the same,
i can't believe one could change me as much as she did,
from a positive bright flower to something that can't even be
described.

Dear Father

You may feel depressed, just to see someone's face filled
with joy and not a bit of disgrace,
a true definition of a man, with one word, is father,
you're a shining armed knight in my sweet dreams followed
by my actual life.
Thank you for being who you are that raised me to believe
no one is more important than family,
you deserve more than you get,
you bring happiness to me and your wife,
you held me tight while I was thinking about something that
night.
I truly love you despite me showing my feelings in different
ways,
fathers deserve more than feelings just like a disgrace,
you work and work just to see a smile and not even a thank
you has been applied,
now it's our time to switch the lights and make you the star
of our day light.

Dad we love you and always will,
being brats, as kids has hidden the fact of who you are and
the love you deserve,
love you forever and never is something that I don't
remember.

17

Fade

Pictures are great because the people in them can change but the memory will never fade.

Day by Day

Day by day my interests in you decrease as the hurtful words
from you increase,
day by day I feel like you aren't a friend to be called,
a person to talk to,
someone, who I can be myself with,
day by day you are losing me the same way you were using
me.
You are losing the person who once loved you,
who once cared for you,
who once gave you a chance to improve,
yet an apology can't come from you,
you are losing a friend that once treated you more
than what she got.

Imperfections Filled My Soul

Trying to run away from what I had been told, but in reality,
its stuck up in my soul,
words can come and go but not yours,
tearing me apart with their sharp edges of truths that
have been told,
nonetheless, thriving through it all,
trying to find it within my soul,
being imperfectly perfect is who I was born to be, and it
is my living reality.
Finding a soul within the depth of my body will take me
through a downfall of a mountain to find dignity in a harsh
place like reality.

Darkness

I was in the third grade when she finally walked away,
she had left me all alone, inside this place, dark and hollow,
feeling scared and sorrow,
like there won't be a tomorrow,
scared of falling in love,
scared to let go but for once I do,
I feel you, I let you go,
now all I want to do is come home, the place that you adore,
a place filled with happiness and joy.

Thank you

After everything, words that come out of your mouth will never be the same. Thanks for all the pain.

Loneliness

Feeling alone here, without you,
is making me want to swallow up all the pieces that
were left behind, with the tone of your voice stuck in my
head,
haunting me with endless memories of you and I.

Learn

Learn from the hated lessons we call mistakes.
It may give you a hard time, but you would be grateful later
on.

Your Happiness

Happiness doesn't revolve around a person but revolves
around the choices we make,
people come and go,
some leave with a note in mind while other repeat the same
mistake twice and thrice till it's over…
They will be left with nothing but teary eyes in a dark night.

Simple Words

Words can't describe how I feel about you, but actions **do**,
loving someone isn't by telling a simple sentence formed by
three words,
it is meaningless, if your actions don't prove your love.

Three Words

I love you, is simply three words forming a sentence,
repeated by many but meant by little,
you can say it but not mean it,
you prove your love with actions, not words that can be
forgotten,
feelings are proven by actions not words.

Lost

Lost in my thoughts,
trying to maintain it all,
finding a way to survive but losing it all,
searching for a clue that's glued to your eyes,
that is shut with curtains opened by one person and one
person only.

Treatment Is Key

Keep treating me the way you do,
when time comes,
I will appear distant,
don't come back and wonder what did you do.
I, as well, am a human being that is capable of feelings the
same as you,
not an animal you can mistreat without caring for.

Kindness

Being kind makes me happy but for you,
it doesn't,
putting me down with my emotions and messing around
with a fragile soul is what pleasures you.

What's Love

Simply thinking your presence is the main reason a person could love you isn't what love is, when your presence, your minds, and souls are connected with one another, that's love.

The Funny Friend

Being the positive friend may have the benefit of being trusted, but it has the disadvantage of being a therapist to many and silenced by more.

We Are All the Same

Are bodies all people can talk about? Skinny, curvy, fat, obese, under or overweight, many different colors and sizes but the mind is being ignored for the rest of what it holds .

Where Are You Now

Your presence is extinct,
your face is hard to remember,
your voice is something I can't recall.
I can see you once in a while and pretend like we are happy,
but lying is the truth of our reality.
We fake our happiness while we ache deep down inside.
Effort is what we need,
your presence is what we need,
it is you who we need.
Day by day, I hate your presence more and more for who
you have become.
Thanks for ruining a relationship that was slowly growing,

Night

In the end, I lay in my bed,
thinking day and night,
what would I be doing if I haven't met you?
Disappointing thoughts surrounding my head,

can't seem to get why I feel so dead.

Pain, Pain, Go Away

Thank you for the unwanted pain, thank you for the endless nights and loss of sleep, thank you for ruining what once was a bloomed flower.

Warrior

I am not living,
I'm surviving a war in a battlefield rephrased as "Planet
Earth,"
I am no human.
I am a survivor.
A warrior.

Fake

Some say aliens aren't real.
How do you explain my friends actions then?
Two-faced, fake, weird and horribly stink
all makes sense to being aliens.
If aliens aren't real, I guess I befriended a bunch of fakes.

Writer

As a kid, she spent her time reading books.
As a teenager, she read even more but started writing.
As an adult, she became a writer.
A writer who writes her thoughts away.

www.ingramcontent.com/pod-product-compliance
Lightning Source LLC
Chambersburg PA
CBHW051403250726
48656CB00006B/2248